Luisa Rose

Eine Blumenhochzeit

Ausmalbuch für Erwachsene

Bibliografische Information der Deutschen Nationalbibliothek:
Die Deutsche Nationalbibliothek verzeichnet diese Publikation in der
Deutschen Nationalbibliografie; detaillierte bibliografische
Daten sind im Internet über http://dnb.dnb.de abrufbar.

© 2016 Luisa Rose; 1. Auflage
Covergrafik, Texte & Illustrationen © 2016 Luisa Rose

Herstellung und Verlag: BoD – Books on Demand, Norderstedt

ISBN: 9783743104105

A·FLOWER·WEDDING

Yes, flower bells rang right merry that day,
When there was a marriage of flowers,
they say.

Young LAD'S LOVE had courted Miss Meadow.
And the two soon agreed at the Altar Sweet,
to meet.

A LILY white robe was worn by the Bride, And SWEET WILLIAM, the Groom, drest in red, at her side.

Miss VIOLET, PRIMROSE, and gay MARYGOLD, With their LADIES' FINGERS her train did uphold.

Whilst her father looked young, though with OLD MAN'S BEARD.

(Was a DANDELION in youth I have heard.)

The troth was plighted for woe or for weal,
And the lines attested by SOLOMON'S SEAL:

The BACHELOR'S BUTTON was cast aside,

And the throng that witnessed was LONDON'S PRIDE:

There was GOOD KING HENRY, & tall JONQUIL,

Like NARCISSUS himself by the waters still;

There were LORDS & LADIES to grace the dance,

And Rosemary, and—

With his Golden Rod

the SWEET SULTAN came:

Lastly, CREEPING JENNY, an elderly dame

To order the feast_there was LING, and HARTSTONGUE,

And Goosefoot with Sage, the House-Leek among

Very Sweet Peas, & Good Cherry Pie,
Such a feast as an Alderman could not deny!

In lovely KING·CUPS there was CHAMOMILE TEA

A nd the fortune in gifts was a wonder to see!
A new PENNY-ROYAL,
A fine GOLDEN FEATHER;

A pair of HORSE-CHESTNUTS,

a JACOB'S LADDER,

Venus's Looking Glass,

a fine ARROW-HEAD
Discovered long since in the river's
bed;

Garments of FLAX,

and a LADY'S CUSHION;

Hose-in-Hose, Lady's Slippers to put on,

Buttercups gold, and a Pitcher-Plant,
Nay, everything that a house could want.

In Venus's Fly-Trap the pair drove away,

"SPEEDWELL, and be happy," their friends gaily say;

But alack! what a hubbub when one chanced to find
The Bride's only BOX was there left behind!

The WILD·THYME they had, and the fuss that was made
Kept the guests in a rout thro' the DEADLY NIGHT SHADE.

But the CLOCKS ticked apace to the ope of DAISY SNOWFLAKES were fast falling when all said good-bye,

Weitere Ausmalbücher von Luisa Rose:

Titel	ISBN
Alice im Wunderland	9783741297502
Blumen und Märchen	9783743102002
Der Struwwelpeter	9783743102699
Die Struwwelliese	9783743102811
Don Quixote	9783743104037
Drei kleine Schweine	9783743104099
Eine Blumenhochzeit	9783743104105
Fröhliche Reigenspiele	9783743104112
Lustige Tanzspiele	9783743104273
Reise ins antike Griechenland	9783743112568
Flucht ins antike Griechenland	9783743112599
Pariser Leben im 19.Jahrhundert	9783743112704
Die Sommerkönigin	9783743112742
Der Schneider und die Krähe	9783743112827
Die Wikinger	9783743113275
Hänsel und Gretel	9783743114265
Max und Moritz	9783743103214
Schnurrdirburr	9783743112834
Mode des 18. und 19. Jahrhunderts	9783743112971
Kostümbilder des 18. und 19. Jahrhunderts	9783743114401
Abenteuer im Bienenland	9783743117051
Griechische Helden der Antike	9783743117709
Märchen alter Zeit	9783743116559

Notizbücher von Luisa Rose:

Titel	ISBN
Drachentöter (Notizbuch)	9783743113077
Natures Wonders (Notizbuch)	9783743113817
Gedankenspiel Notizen (Notizbuch)	9783743113886
Smaragd Notizen (Notizbuch)	9783743114296
Jagd Notizen (Notizbuch)	9783743114302
Tradition (Notizbuch)	9783743114319
Antik Notizbuch (Notizbuch)	9783743114326
Veni Vidi Vici (Notizbuch)	9783743114340
Black List (Notizbuch)	9783743114371
Mystic Notes (Notizbuch)	9783743114388
Magic Notes (Notizbuch)	9783743114418
Fantasien (Notizbuch)	9783743114463
Creative Notes (Notizbuch)	9783743114487
Persönliche Notizen (Notizbuch)	9783743114494
Peter Pan (Notizbuch)	9783743114531
Rose (Notizbuch)	9783743114548
Quality Street (Notizbuch)	9783743114555
Rubin Notizen (Notizbuch)	9783743114647
Schmetterlinge (Notizbuch)	9783743114661
Ali Baba (Notizbuch)	9783743114678
The portrait of a Lady (Notizbuch)	9783743114692
Shakespeare (Notizbuch)	9783743114722
Brainstorming (Notizbuch)	9783743114739
Merlin (Notizbuch)	9783743114746
Rügen (Notizbuch)	9783743114784

Möchtest du über neue Bücher von Luisa Rose per email Informiert werden? Dann schicke eine Email mit ‚Newsletter' im Betreff an Luisa.Rose@t-online.de